Shadow Catch

ALSO BY DAPHNE MARLATT

POETRY AND PROSE POETRY

Between Brush Strokes (with book design and drawings by Frances Hunter)
Character / Jeu de lettres (with Nicole Brossard)
Double Negative (with Betsy Warland)
Frames of a Story
The Given
Here & There
Intertidal: The Collected Earlier Poems, 1968–2008 (edited by Susan Holbrook)*
leaf leaf/s
Liquidities: Vancouver Poems Then and Now
Mauve (with Nicole Brossard)
Our Lives
*Reading Sveva**
Rings
Rivering: The Poetry of Daphne Marlatt (edited by Susan Knutson)
Seven Glass Bowls
Steveston (with photographs by Robert Minden)
*Then Now**
*This Tremor Love Is**
Touch to My Tongue (with artwork by Cheryl Sourkes)
Vancouver Poems
Winter / Rice / Tea Strain

PROSE AND POETRY

At the River's Mouth: Writing Migrations
Ghost Works
How Hug a Stone
Net Work: Selected Writing (edited by Fred Wah)*
Readings from the Labyrinth
Salvage

The Story, She Said (with George Bowering, Brian Fawcett, Dwight Gardiner, Gladys Hindmarch, Roy Kiyooka, Gerry Gilbert, and Carole Itter)
Two Women in a Birth (with Betsy Warland)
What Matters: Writing, 1968–70

FICTION

Ana Historic
Taken
Zócalo

DRAMA

The Gull (translated by Toyoshi Yoshihara)*

COLLECTIONS EDITED

In the Feminine: Women and Words / Les femmes et les mots: Conference Proceedings, 1983 (with Ann Dybikowski, Victoria Freeman, Barbara Pulling, and Betsy Warland)
Lost Language: Selected Poems of Maxine Gadd (with Ingrid Klassen)
Mother Talk: The Life-Stories of Mary Kiyoshi Kiyooka (by Roy Kiyooka, posthumous)
Opening Doors: Vancouver's East End (with Carole Itter)
Steveston Recollected: A Japanese-Canadian History (with translation by Maya Koizumi)
Telling It: Women and Language across Cultures (with SKY Lee, Lee Maracle, and Betsy Warland)

* Published by Talonbooks

Shadow Catch

A Chamber Opera Libretto

Daphne Marlatt

Talonbooks

Talonbooks
9259 Shaughnessy Street, Vancouver, British Columbia, Canada V6P 6R4
talonbooks.com

Talonbooks is located on xʷməθkʷəy̓əm, Sḵwx̱wú7mesh, and səl̓ilwətaʔɬ Lands.

First printing: 2023

Typeset in Minion
Printed and bound in Canada on 100% post-consumer recycled paper

Interior and cover design by Typesmith
Cover photographs by Sarah Race

Talonbooks acknowledges the financial support of the Canada Council for the Arts, the Government of Canada through the Canada Book Fund, and the Province of British Columbia through the British Columbia Arts Council and the Book Publishing Tax Credit.

Rights to produce *Shadow Catch*, in whole or in part, in any medium by any group, amateur or professional, are retained by the librettist and composers. Interested persons are requested to contact them care of Talonbooks.

Library and Archives Canada Cataloguing in Publication

Title: Shadow catch / Daphne Marlatt
Names: Marlatt, Daphne, author.
Identifiers: Canadiana 20220430594 | ISBN 9781772015225 (softcover)
Subjects: LCSH: Operas—Librettos. | LCSH: Vancouver (B.C.)—History—Drama.
Classification: LCC ML50 M347 S52 2022 | DDC C812/.6—dc23

for Colleen Lanki

for her years of Noh theatre work in Vancouver

"A Noh play ... is not the telling of a
series of events but an exploration,
an evocation, and indeed a song of praise."

—KUNIO KOMPARU
The Noh Theater: Principles and Perspectives,
translated by Jane Corddry (1980)

The Making of *Shadow Catch*

Poets aren't usually asked to write librettos. I knew Vancouver poet Robin Blaser had written the libretto for Sir Harrison Birtwhistle's opera *The Last Supper* (2000), but that was the only recent exception I was aware of. So I was surprised when, in late 2010, I was approached by composer Benton Roark with a very particular request. He and three other Vancouver composers were thinking about composing music for a chamber opera influenced by classical Japanese Noh theatre and they asked me if I would be interested in writing a libretto for it.

This was a challenge: How Noh-like could a chamber opera for Western music be? Noh is a classical form of Japanese poetic theatre and dance with a centuries-old tradition. I had previously written a Canadian version of a Noh play, *The Gull*, produced by Vancouver's Pangaea Arts in a cross-cultural production in Richmond, BC, in 2006 under the direction of Noh maestro and composer Richard Emmert. It starred Akira Matsui, an eminent Kita-school performer from Wakayama alongside Canadian actors and Japanese Noh musicians. This, however, would be quite a different project. For one thing, Noh has a basic two-act structure, essential for its storyline, but this libretto would require four acts, although it would still need to show Noh influence. Benton had studied with Colleen Lanki of TomoeArts, who herself had studied Noh theatre under Richard Emmert in Japan and was well trained in other forms of classical Japanese dance. Colleen would become the director of this project and my dramaturge.

How put together four different acts, each with music by a different composer, and somehow make it Noh-like? Setting can be very significant in one form of classical Noh that stages the arrival of a traveller at a site where some previous traumatic event keeps a spirit repeating that event by recounting it. I felt that choosing a setting that reflects some of our city's history, especially its Japanese Canadian history, would help to unify the individual acts. Vancouver's Downtown Eastside Oppenheimer Park was an obvious choice. Oppenheimer is a well-used, tree-lined park with a double row of cherry trees planted to honour the pre-war Japanese Canadian community that once flourished around it. The park is a site of Indigenous cultural claims and more recently a refuge for people living on the street. Originally known as Powell Street Grounds, it was a stump-cleared area designated in 1902 as the first sports ground of what would become an ethnically diverse city. By the 1920s it was the beating heart of Paueru Gai, the area along Powell Street that, from the 1890s on, was home to the early Japanese Canadian community with its tea houses, bathhouses, tofu and grocery shops. This was a thriving community before the government-enforced exile and internment of Japanese Canadian citizens during WW II. And in the 1920s and 1930s it was known as home base for the well-loved Asahi baseball team, which went on to win many league championships before internment broke the team apart along with their community.

Many of Nihonmachi's early residents worked at Hastings Mill, the sawmill that began what would become the city of Vancouver. In 1865 that mill's predecessor, Stamp's Mill, was built on the wooded peninsula then known as K'emk'emeláy̓, a grove of flourishing bigleaf maple trees blessed with salmon streams and often used as a campsite by Sḵwx̱wú7mesh (Squamish) and x̱ʷməθkʷəy̓əm (Musqueam) Peoples fishing and gathering there. Now heavily industrialized, it is merely a part of Vancouver's extensive dock area, those once-giant maple trees logged for nineteenth-century lumber.

So it felt appropriate to begin the libretto with the ghostly presence of those maple trees as the setting for act 1. The Asahi ball team and its last pre-internment game on Powell Street Grounds in Paueru Gai form the setting for act 2. Act 3 takes its inspiration from Vancouver's early red-light district, a series of brothels in well-furnished houses on 500–600 Alexander Street, one block north of Powell Street, near the waterfront. The tiled entrance to one of those substantial houses still bore the madam's name when Curt Lang photographed it in 1972.*

The fourth act is based on the history of protest in Oppenheimer Park, the only park in the city where demonstrations and protests were allowed during the Depression. There was often violence from the police as well as from demonstrators, the worst incident being the 1935 Ballantyne Pier dockworkers' strike, when mounted police clubbed protestors back from the docks and into the neighbourhood. For many years, Vancouver police had a history of accepting bribes, being "on the take," right into the 1950s, culminating in the Mulligan Affair. The policeman in act 4 is one of these corrupt officers, and in his encounter with him the young runaway recognizes echoes of the violence he experienced at the hands of his dad.

Structure

Having four different composers led me to think about the five traditional categories of Noh plays (god, warrior, woman, lunatic, demon) that would be performed in sequence during a daylong program. I chose mugen Noh, or spirit Noh, as my character guide, which meant that the shite in each act would be a ghost. However, *Shadow Catch* departs from the traditional structure of Noh in a major way. In Noh, the major performer is the shite, who interacts with the waki or secondary performer. The waki, often a traveller who arrives at a place that is the site of a traumatic past event for the shite, acts as a listener or questioner who draws out the shite's story and in so doing releases that spirit from whatever obsession or passion they have been tied to. But *Shadow Catch* features the story of a different shite in each act who engages with the same

---

* The publisher was denied permission to reproduce Curt Lang's photograph in this book. However, it can be viewed in the Vancouver Public Library's Historical Photographs collection, www.vpl.ca/historicalphotos, accession number: 85872X.

waki through all four acts. In this way its overall story becomes the story of the waki, a runaway boy who is released from his fear by visitations from successive ghost-shites. Each of them has something to tell him about the history of the area in which he is trying to fall asleep and forget about what he's run from, and each shite has their own psychological knot. By the end of the opera, the boy has realized not only the history of where he's found himself but a fuller sense of who he is.

Poetic Language

Noh theatre developed from the classical tradition of Japanese poetry or waka. As a form of poetic theatre, its strongly dramatic components are expressed in music and dance as well as in sung and spoken lines. This libretto would not include dance, but it would still include sequences of poetic lines. Japanese is a syllabic language so tanka, the poetic form basic to Noh, is written in a count of 5-7-5-7-7 syllable lines. English poetry is usually based on a rhythm of spoken word accents, not syllables, so the waka form can often feel confining for writers working in English. The poetic lines of *Shadow Catch* vary between 6, 3, 5, and 7 or more syllables modified by word stress, while prose occurs in the conversational passages.

Organization

We began some time in 2010 with a series of meetings between myself, Colleen Lanki, and the four composers, Dorothy Chang, Benton Roark, Jennifer Butler, and Farshid Samandari (listed here in the order of their acts). I outlined my idea of setting it in Oppenheimer Park and in some of the history around the old Powell Street Grounds, and then with their approval began writing. Early in 2011, we came together for a brief intensive workshop with David Crandall of Theatre Nohgaku in the US, himself a well-trained Noh performer, composer, and playwright.

Once we had scores and libretto, and each composer had chosen her or his act, the long process of auditions began. Noh plays call for four musicians who perform onstage on three different kinds of drums and a bamboo (Noh) flute. Our chamber opera hired three Vancouver musicians: cellist Lee Duckles, flautist Mark Takeshi McGregor, and percussionist Brian Nesselroad. Marguerite Witvoet came on board as musical director and everyone worked hard during rehearsals. This was very much a collaborative venture under the sponsorship of Vancouver Pro Musica and TomoeArts.

The Firehall Arts Centre, only a block from Oppenheimer Park, seemed the perfect venue and Donna Spencer, a Firehall founding director, welcomed us. *Shadow Catch* was produced and performed there late in 2011 with spare sets designed by Yulia Shtern and historical photographs projected onstage by Craig Alfredson. The program included some informative statements. What follows are excerpts.

From Producer Benton Roark

Years ago I discussed with Colleen Lanki and Mark McGregor the possibility of transporting the expression and colour of contemporary music into the mysterious and refined world of Noh theatre. Having an intuition that both genres' abstract tendencies (organized sound in the one; distillment, symbolism, and poetry in the other) would meet in a level and fruitful way, I began to walk this interdisciplinary path with zeal. It wasn't long before I realized how well trodden it had already become since the Eastern leanings of the early twentieth-century modernists. On my own path, my strong desire for cultural awareness and respect for tradition began to give me some hesitancy. But when Farshid Samandari suggested (quite out of the blue) approaching Vancouver Pro Musica's Further East / Further West series with a proposal for a Noh-based project, and when quickly thereafter Daphne Marlatt (who recently had won the Uchimura Naoya Prize for her Noh play *The Gull*) agreed to consider writing for it, I started to realize that these two traditions still might find a lot to talk about! More importantly, perhaps, a group had already started to assemble – Colleen, Daphne, Farshid, Dorothy Chang, Jennifer Butler, Marguerite Witvoet, and myself – that could address these questions with experience, sensitivity, and a spirit of wonder.

From Composers Dorothy Chang, Benton Roark, Jennifer Butler, and Farshid Samandari

With composers being used to having ultimate control over their own music, it was an unusual experience to have to consider how our acts would fit into a cohesive musical whole – an exceptionally difficult challenge, given that no one had a clear sense of what that cohesive whole would be! We composers met frequently for discussion, negotiation, and coordination of everything ranging from the necessity (or lack thereof?) of a five-octave marimba, to the level of chromaticism in the waki's musical lines, to the consistent notation of *Sprechstimme* in each act. These sessions kept us more or less on the same creative page as we journeyed together through the process of composing a collaborative opera.

From Director Colleen Lanki

We are not using Noh instruments, masks, or costumes, and the performers do not move to Noh music, yet I have tried to imbue this piece with what I think is the essence of Noh.

First of all, Memory. The play is about memory and the reliving of critical personal events in order to be able to move on.

Then there are Time and Space. Noh space/time extends, contracts, and may even stop. This two-hour performance takes place both in a single night and over "generations generous."

Finally, there is *Yūgen*, a Noh theatre aesthetic that roughly translates as "mysterious grace." In this world all things have a kind of half-hidden beauty and even a demon holds a branch of flowers.

Noh opens up a world of shadows we must face before we can move on, and *Shadow Catch* introduces us to a few of the spirits that wander through Vancouver every day, who have made us who we are.

* * *

That seemed the end of an unusual venture, but a decade later Colleen Lanki and I heard from Dorothy Chang that Nancy Hermiston, director of the UBC Opera Ensemble, was planning to remount *Shadow Catch* in March 2022. Nancy had been in the audience for one of the Firehall performances and had seen the chamber opera as a dramatic way to feature the significant history of Oppenheimer Park. Further research went into the UBC production, including an interview with Kaye Kaminishi, surviving member of the Asahi baseball team, and a talk to the cast by xʷməθkʷəy̓əm Elder Larry Grant. The program for this production featured excellent articles on the history generating each act: the Indigenous history of the park right up to the present; a brief history of the Asahi ball team, originally formed in 1914; a very brief history of Vancouver's early red-light district; and an account of the waterfront strikes that culminated in the Battle of Ballantyne Pier in 1935. The UBC production was performed by a talented, mainly student cast in a full set featuring several upright and fallen tree trunks as the park. Carefully selected historical photographs from the Vancouver Public Library archives and the city's Historical Archives were projected on the rear of the stage during each act. Under Nancy Hermiston's direction, and with conductor Jonathan Girard, a cast of convincing student actors drawn from the UBC Opera Ensemble, and three professional musicians, flautist Paolo Bortolussi, cellist Sungyong Lim, and percussionist Brian Nesselroad, *Shadow Catch* was dramatically staged as a westernized chamber opera in the Old Auditorium at UBC.

—DAPHNE MARLATT

August 2020

Shadow Catch

Production History

Shadow Catch was first produced from December 2 to 4, 2011, at the Firehall Theatre as part of Vancouver Pro Musica's Further East / Further West series and the City of Vancouver's 125th anniversary celebration, with the following cast and crew:

WAKI	Joseph Bulman
SHITE	
SPIRIT OF THE MAPLE TREES	Melanie Adams
SPIRIT OF THE ASAHI BASEBALL PLAYER	Michael Mori
SPIRIT OF THE BROTHEL MADAM	Margo LeVae
SPIRIT OF THE POLICE OFFICER	Lawrence Cotton

Flute	Mark McGregor
Cello	Lee Duckles
Percussion	Brian Nesselroad
Direction and Choreography	Colleen Lanki
Musical Direction	Marguerite Witvoet

Characters

WAKI: the runaway

SHITE: a spirit, different in each act, each performed by a separate singer

> In act 1, **SHITE** is the **SPIRIT OF THE MAPLE TREES.**

> In act 2, **SHITE** is the **SPIRIT OF THE ASAHI BASEBALL PLAYER.**

> In act 3, **SHITE** is the **SPIRIT OF THE BROTHEL MADAM.**

> In act 4, **SHITE** is the **SPIRIT OF THE POLICE OFFICER.**

JI: the chorus, made up of the remaining three **SHITE** in each act

Setting

Oppenheimer Park, Vancouver, BC

Joseph Bulman as the Waki in *Shadow Catch* at the Firehall Theatre, December 2011.

Photo by Timothy Matheson.

Michael Mori as the Spirit of the Asahi Baseball Player, with Margo LeVae as the Spirit of the Brothel Madam, Lawrence Cotton as the Spirit of the Police Officer, and Melanie Adams as the Spirit of the Maple Trees in *Shadow Catch* at the Firehall Theatre, December 2011.

Photo by Timothy Matheson.

Margo LeVae as the Spirit of the Brothel Madam in *Shadow Catch* at the Firehall Theatre, December 2011.

Photo by Timothy Matheson.

Melanie Adams as the Spirit of the Maple Trees in *Shadow Catch* at the Firehall Theatre, December 2011.

Photo by Timothy Matheson.

Act 1

SHITE

Spirit of the Maple Trees

Composer: Dorothy Chang

Score in C

(divide SATB chorus
by range; can alter
throughout as needed)

S H A D O W   C A T C H
Act I

Daphne Marlatt

Dorothy Chang

*Oppenheimer Park: summer. Three members of The Chorus
are seated on a park bench with the Tree Spirit perched on a
stump beside the bench. From the Tree Spirit's hands a giant maple leaf,
looking almost like a fan, dangles by her knees.*

Oppenheimer Park. Summer. JI are seated
on a park bench with SHITE perched on an
upside-down garbage can beside the bench.
From SHITE's hands a giant maple leaf, looking
almost like a fan, dangles between her knees.

Instrumental passage. JI begins chanting.

JI

K'emk'emeláẏ
Paueru Groundo
Oppenheimer
Powell Street Grounds
Hastings Reserve

K'emk'emeláẏ
Paueru Groundo
Oppenheimer
Powell Street Grounds
Hastings Reserve

the nameless rhythm ground
of those long gone and here

Entrance music for WAKI.

WAKI enters as a tired teenage runaway coming
into the park for the first time. He wears a hoodie
and carries a small pack. He looks around fearfully
as he makes his way down the park pathway.

WAKI

This block's dim grass unfenced
shabby trees a park
they said to sleep where shadow
bodies lie

JI

To sleep where shadow bodies lie

WAKI

Or yell out anger dreams but I
will take street light to be
a safer house tonight.

Self-declaration.

WAKI

I am a boy who was given up. My dad in the slammer, Mom
gone, social workers took me to a foster home in a small
town. There I was kicked around, the kid in trouble, who
didn't belong.

Travel song.

WAKI

Slipping out unseen at night
I left that false home
the hands of those who hate.
Fourteen now

I know the curse behind the eyes
of the angel face
the mouth that smiles then
fucks you up. No more.
No thanks. Trudging and hitching
my way to Vancouver
I've arrived at high-rise hope
at some new chance – if I
can find somewhere to sleep
some place that might
feel safe –

This doorway's taken
someone growled at me.

JI

This doorway's taken.
Go find your own place.

WAKI

Now I've found this shabby park, I'll settle some distance
away from those others doing who knows what in the city-
dark. Here's a tree that looks safe and it's quiet enough. I'll
try to sleep.

> *WAKI settles himself to sleep. Silence.*
>
> *SHITE, appearing as a middle-aged street
> person, starts to walk down the path towards
> WAKI while fanning herself with her leaf.*
>
> *Spoken dialogue.*

SHITE

(*in a low voice*) Now what's that kid doing here in "Hastings Reserve"? Maybe wants a bit of party action, eh?

> *SHITE leans over the sleeping WAKI and tickles him with her leaf, then jumps quickly behind his tree. WAKI starts up, flinging out an arm in frightened self-defence.*

WAKI

Who poked me? Someone poked me. Someone or some thing – a needle?

> *WAKI checks his arms, then kneels to frantically search the ground.*

I don't see anything. (*looking around*) And no one near enough.

SHITE

No one you saw, boy. But you can hear, can't you?

WAKI

Who's that? (*looking behind him at JI*) Not those guys partying by the old backstop. They're still there, it can't be them.

SHITE

(*coming out from behind the boy's tree*) I might be them,
might be any one of you sitting on your ass in a shabby park –
you said "shabby," didn't you? Let me tell you, those three are
having more than a shabby time. Open your ears, kid. Listen
to them laugh.

WAKI

(*jumping up*) Who the hell are you?

SHITE

You want to know what's what when you can't even hear
what's around you. Hell, is it? – That's *your* idea.

WAKI

Oh yeah? You don't look too good yourself.

SHITE

Looking, always looking. Why don't you listen?
Open your ears, you might hear
how the trees stand in
their shadows of yesteryear,
each one murmuring,

SHITE and **JI**

(*softly*) Be here! Be here!

SHITE

(*loudly again*) Ha! Well you can't hear past your own self, eh? Too bad. You don't hear what the leaves have to say.

WAKI

Are you crazy? Trees don't talk.

SHITE

Not in your world. But you're in ours now, kid. Do you have any idea where you are?

WAKI

(*sitting down, mumbling*) Okay, okay. I don't know what you're on about. Just leave me alone.

> *WAKI pulls up his hoodie and turns away, curled into himself.*
>
> *Introductory song for* SHITE, *who transforms into the Spirit of the Maple Trees that once flourished in K'emk'emeláy̓ in pre-contact time.*

SHITE

Leave, you say? No sleep for you
when it's the past you've
parked your sorry body in.

JI

Listen to the wind
the leavings of all the years...

SHITE

Listen and you'll hear
the Old Ones inter-leafing here...

WAKI

(*mumbling*) Leave me alone.

> *WAKI nods off. SHITE begins to transform the*
> *space into a pre-contact maple grove.*

SHITE

You're in deep now, kid,
deep shawl of leaves, this grove of
bigleaf maples so
much larger than you can see
here in K'emk'emeláy̓.

> *Tree song.*

SHITE and **JI**

Between these interlaced and
whispering leaves,
hand talk with wind, outstretched and
offering inter-speak
with passing cloud and rain for
generations generous.

SHITE

Hear cautious feet
deer shuffle in
shadows, a knock-
knock-knock, no
flicker thinks it's *his*
ridged bark that
tree frog climbs –

SHITE and **JI**

The rise and fall of song's
wash ever-tidal wave
so intertempo'd here.

> *SHITE moves towards WAKI and*
> *bends over him.*

SHITE

Can you hear?
From your separate hell
can you hear my hello?

> *SHITE sweeps one hand over the sleeping*
> *WAKI's body with no response from him.*

SHITE

We'll leaf-talk then.

> *Memory song, slow and reminiscent at first.*

SHITE and **JI**

> Moon, sap, rain
> relations untold, unnamed,
> 'til human tellers gave
> their word to us,
> K'emk'emeláy̓

SHITE

> Here we stood,
> here we flourished,

SHITE and **JI**

> Windstrung, sung
> let go, re-flourished
> countless green hellos
> in the interspecies song
> this rhythm ground…

> *Sound of a sharp blow on wood. **SHITE** stops,*
> *looks back at **WAKI**, who stirs fitfully but does*
> *not come fully awake.*

SHITE

> Hear that noise?
> It's the shock of a clock
> the run-in on time.

SHITE and **JI**

> Others came with axes,
> saws, thudded us down,
> deaf to all but the roaring mills

their tallies, their hours,
their rising profits they stole
and stacked us up, dead,

SHITE stops moving.

SHITE

Dead and deaf.

*SHITE becomes an ordinary street person again.
She turns to walk back towards the JI bench as
WAKI rises, sleepwalking, one arm slowly lifting
towards her.*

WAKI

Don't... don't...

SHITE stops, turns back.

SHITE

You do hear, then?

*WAKI stands silent, still asleep, his arm
slowly dropping.*

SHITE

Perhaps not. We've run out of time.

SHITE turns away towards the JI bench.

Instrumental music. SHITE sits on the JI bench. WAKI, half asleep, slowly folds back into his resting spot.

JI

And leaving leave
only leaf splatter, leaf
patter in your ear.

WAKI jerks awake and looks around as if he had missed something.

Act 2

SHITE

Spirit of the
Asahi Baseball Player

Composer: Benton Roark

Instrumental music. WAKI is seated at his spot
downstage from JI, looking around him.

Waiting song.

WAKI

I found a place in this park
but what kind of place?
Who was that who appeared to me
in the shadow night?
Strange dream or some old spirit
of this weird place?

JI

This weird place.

WAKI

Where sleepless folk hang high
and not at all dry.
They shout, they mumble, they drum up
monsters, tree spirits
fall from the leaves to startle
visitors like me –

Now a humming, now some weirdo
coming, I don't want
trouble, don't want any drugs.

Entrance music. SHITE wanders down the park
pathway, appearing as an old park cleaner in
faded Asahi baseball cap and dirty coveralls.
He is stooped in posture and stabs at invisible
litter with a pronged stick.

Entrance song.

SHITE

Bright as it was once,
sunstruck and quick, sharp crack of
the hit, the leap to
catch it, gone – long gone –
All glory only
a moment in the blink
of an eye.
This ground so worn now, litter
everywhere I walk I gather
leftover bits of
transient lives left too
suddenly behind.

JI

Scattered we were –
some here, some there.

SHITE

Night after night I
wander faded through the leaves
to pick up scattered
pieces left by other lives.

WAKI

That old guy is stabbing up each piece of garbage as if it were
alive. He must be the park cleaner but why does he work
at night?

SHITE

Catch it, catch it before it
zings on past my out-
stretched hand – He's
out!

Now we're up, we're up
before their eyes in smoke-blue
mountain twilight
under ever-changing sky
we run, we slide –

JI

Homing, homing in
on the dark that hovers just
outside.

> *SHITE has approached WAKI and stabs at
> his pack beside him. WAKI leaps to his feet,
> dragging his pack away.*
>
> *Spoken dialogue, with some chanting.*

WAKI

What are you doing? That's my pack.

SHITE

Sorry, so sorry. I was somewhere else. Or maybe I was here and you were somewhere else.

WAKI

That doesn't make any sense.

SHITE

At times it's hard to see
the sense in what's real.

WAKI

Look, I find a place to sleep, then you come along and stab my pack. Why don't you work by daylight when it's easier to see what belongs to people?

SHITE

What belongs, you say, and to whom? We thought Paueru Groundo was ours, we thought our houses, the Buddhist temple, our school, our shops, the noodle and tofu makers, this baseball diamond, all that we worked so hard to make was ours. Then Pearl Harbour happened and overnight we learned none of it was.

WAKI

Wait a minute. Pearl Harbour was ... last century? World War II or something. You can't be that old.

> *SHITE begins to transform into a young*
> *ball player in the next five lines, but then*

reverts to stooped cleaner again when WAKI
challenges him.

SHITE

We are the young new ones
on the team, we are
salmon leaping for the cup,
we are shooting stars
in the last game played right here.

WAKI

Come on! You played ball here? In this one-block park?

SHITE

You don't know much.

WAKI

I know what I've run from.

SHITE

That's never enough.

> *The next four lines are chanted like a*
> *team chant.*

JI

You sleep on Paueru Groundo,

SHITE

Home ground for the Asahi,

JI

One, two, three! Most popular ball team,

SHITE

In the city,

JI

Before the war
broke up the team interned in
scattered camps inland
some here, some there.

SHITE

We never stopped playing, we trained new young ones but the
news forgot us, wrote us off as if we were dead.

WAKI

That's too bad but it happened long ago. Why are you telling
me now?

> *SHITE stands erect now in his glory as a young
> Asahi ball player miming the actions he sings.*
>
> *Memory song.*

SHITE

This field is where it happens
over and over.
Benches packed, bases loaded.
Out in left field
cheering spectators part for
Frank's brilliant catch.
Five-footers all, we leap, we
catch, and when we're up
we bunt, Harry's suicide squeeze.
We win again, against
long-legged big-hitter teams,
they don't run so fast.
And our fans clap, hakujin too
all recognize true
Yamato-damashii, true
excelling for love
of the game.

JI

Team caps, team uniforms'
white shine, naphtha-scrubbed
by ardent sisters, New Pier
Café jokes and
rivalries for girls eager
to dance, to grace
Belcarra picnics on a
star player's arm,
twilight closing in.

SHITE

We worked days for our
dads when not in school, we hauled

miso tubs, hundred-
pound sacks of rice, unloaded
truckloads of cans, before
and after practice we
lived for the game.

WAKI

So long ago –

SHITE

We lived inside that glory,
local stars we were,
shooting through the unseen dark
fear clouds massing
out beyond the field where we
played ball, bright ball.

> *SHITE pauses as if struck by a further memory.*

JI

Night's dark, the boy thinks,
outside his bright talk, maybe
inside it too.

WAKI

Here's something I've learned:
to move on you have to leave
some things behind.

SHITE

You're young, you don't know
some things don't get left behind.

JI

Our caps, our uniforms we packed
with us to the camps –

SHITE

Even my leap in the last game,
I took it with me.

Instrumental music.

JI

Twilight closing in
end of the season, end of
life's game against all
odds, our star ascent, the ball
at its peak, falling –

SHITE

Bases loaded, he leaps!
Small salmon thrash
against blue mountains'
massive dark – he leaps! –

JI

He misses – oh, he
fumbled the catch!

Oh shame! in the last
inning of the last game.

> SHITE *turns away, crushed. An imaginary*
> *baseball rolls onto the stage at* WAKI's *feet.*
> WAKI *picks it up and turns it over in his hands*
> *in wonder.*

WAKI

A baseball? Here?

SHITE

I can't forget, can't
forget, the shame of it
shadows me here.

WAKI

Hey!

> SHITE *turns quickly.* WAKI *looks at him and*
> *then begins to mime a pitch windup.*

WAKI

Catch!

> He throws the ball to SHITE, *who catches it and*
> *dances a celebratory series of steps, then stops as*
> *if struck by further thought.*

SHITE

A shadow catch.

> *Instrumental music. SHITE slowly sets the*
> *imaginary ball down on the stage, resumes*
> *his form as park cleaner, and shuffles to the JI*
> *bench, where he takes his seat.*

JI

The catch in the dream real:
there is no ball, and yet
the game plays on, plays on ...

> *WAKI looks around him, shrugs, and sits down.*

WAKI

Whose dream was that? Was I
in his? Or was he in mine?
I'm too tired to think.

> *WAKI curls up by his tree to sleep.*

JI

This park, this ground so
thick with dreams of other lives
is where the boy
waking sleeps and sleeping
awakes.

Act 3

SHITE

Spirit of the Brothel Madam

Composer: Jennifer Butler

Instrumental music. WAKI is asleep in his usual
spot. He stirs and then sits up to think.

Waiting song.

WAKI

I thought this dark night park would
hide me, free to be
among nameless people
having no bed, no home
to call their own, nor do I.

JI

No home to call their own.

WAKI

I thought I could be free alone
yet they insist on
telling me how this was home
to them and then,
like passing shadows they're gone,
a gust of words...

JI

A still-repeating memory.

WAKI

I don't want to remember
I will never long for
anything I've left behind.

> *Entrance music. Enter* SHITE, *a blind woman,*
> *elegantly dressed but groping her way along the*
> *path with the help of a cane.*

> *Entrance song.*

SHITE

Help me along, girl,
the path is rough, Powell Ground
so full of lay-abouts.
In my day people had a bed,
maybe a small room
in premises like ours. My rooms
were always clean and
my girls too – I made sure of that.

WAKI

Now who is this blind
woman? Yet another crazy
person talking to herself.

SHITE

Beauty is as beauty does,
they say – nonsense.
Beauty compels us like moths
to a lamp. She was

light on her feet, a delight
and luminous we said,
her skin like sakura
blossom on a thin
rice-paper shade. But she
could lure any man – you laugh?
Just wait – show me where
they put down roots, your cherry trees.

Spoken dialogue.

WAKI

What is she going on about? Old bag. Keep your memories to
yourself, I want to sleep.

SHITE

You are rude, young man. My eyes are dim but I can tell by
your voice how young you are.

WAKI

Look, I don't want trouble...

SHITE

There's no use telling me to look, I cannot see. And as for
looks, well I used to get them, and I used to have them
too. But now it is all too late, and we are looking for the
sakura trees.

WAKI

I don't know anything about that. You look to me like an old
woman bent on bending my ear.

SHITE

An honest voice. You haven't been here long, have you?

WAKI

No, I've come from a small town. No one knows me here and
I like it that way.

SHITE

Ah, so you want to start over? But, like any of us, you come
dragging your shadow behind you.

WAKI

What are you talking about? You just told me you can't see.

SHITE's song of regret. She moves hesitantly,
glancing about as if looking for something
or someone.

SHITE

Powell Ground so changed, street lights
too bright for dimming
eyes see shadows everywhere
this park so full of
sorrow-beings – and I am one.

WAKI

(*exasperated*) One more! Once again!

SHITE

Show me, girl, where are the
sakura trees you told me about?
Roots are a marvel,
a difficult mystery.

JI

A petal foam, a mist
returns each spring surpassing
these our passing lives.

SHITE

But not our shadows, girl,
these shadows we drag
along with us, attached –

JI

I was beautiful
once, so was she.
I was thoughtless once
too many times ...

Spoken dialogue.

WAKI

Excuse me, but who is this girl you keep talking to? I don't
see anyone.

43

SHITE

You haven't developed your eyes, young man.

WAKI

There's nothing wrong with my eyes. There is no one with you, no one at all.

SHITE

She is always with me. Although I did once let her go ...
Oh the once, the once we think has no consequence.

WAKI

I give up trying to sleep. What is this "once"?

> *Memory song. SHITE stands up as a capable*
> *young madam of a 1920s brothel.*

SHITE

Not far from this park
only two short blocks away
stood a house lavish
with rugs, expensive sofas,
beaded lamps, comfortable
rooms for the girls, all six of them
young and alluring,
various types for men with
various appetites.

The pearl of them all was Kiyo
my girl from Kyoto.

JI

Light on her feet, a delight
and luminous we said,
her skin like sakura
blossom on a thin
rice-paper shade...

WAKI's interest is aroused and he interrupts.

Spoken dialogue.

WAKI

She sounds exotic, this pearl. I wouldn't mind seeing
her myself.

SHITE

Exotic, you say? Not to me. Everyone worked and so did we.
We were accepted here, people would nod to me on the street
because I kept a respectable house. Once Kiyo was used to
our life she called my place her home.

*Brief instrumental music. WAKI and SHITE
stand still. JI sings as Kiyo in a soft high voice.*

JI

Alice, you want to see
where they planted the
sakura trees?

*Pause as WAKI and SHITE both
listen for more.*

WAKI

Was that her then? Her voice?

SHITE

At least you have ears.

WAKI

Why does she talk about sakura trees?

SHITE's memory song continues.

SHITE

This is what she would have planted
if she had grown old.
This is what the old ones planted
later, on their return,
to celebrate being rooted here
despite all odds – oh
the odds – why do I use that word?
It wasn't random –
I knew the likely consequence.

JI

Transplant, living bud
encased between glass walls
yet blossoming, her soft allure
drew me, drew any man.

SHITE

Only sixteen –
what did she know of this world
its power-hungry men
who sweet-talk women even
while they despise their
weakness, despise their own
need for them.

WAKI

Despise anyone
they can crush…

SHITE

I knew I should protect her
but love shot through
with jealousy collapses
in the end. I let her go.

JI

(*as Kiyo*) Alice, the sakura trees…

WAKI

You let her go with him?

JI

She believed his sweet talk, she
thought she could just walk
into the better life he painted
with his lying words –

Like a bad dream, a petal
crushed in pelting rain, her body
found not far from here.

WAKI

You let her go!

JI

(*as Kiyo*) The trees, just look at them
abloom in this dark light ...

SHITE

I can't forget I turned
my back and now can't face
this shadow I drag,
always I drag this shadow
along with me.

> *Instrumental refrain of Kiyo's voice.*

WAKI

There's her voice again.

JI

(*as Kiyo*) The sakura trees, dear Alice
are radiant
in evening light, by dim
street light –

SHITE turns to face JI.

SHITE

Kiyo? Kiyo?
Can you forgive me?

JI

(*as Kiyo*) Crossed with shadow, still
they glow and even so I see
our lives, dear Alice,
yours and mine, intertwined.

> *Brief instrumental music. SHITE leans on her
> stick, again a blind old woman.*

SHITE

She tells me and I see
what she can see, our transient
lives so interwound
my shadow, blind, stops here and I
pass on.

> *Brief instrumental music. SHITE walks slowly
> to the JI bench and sits.*

JI

Disappeared like the others –
a dream perhaps?

WAKI

That woman turned to face
the shadow haunting her
and found release. But mine?
But mine?

JI

And now he dare not sleep.

*WAKI moves back to his spot, sitting up
wide awake.*

Act 4

SHITE

Spirit of the Police Officer

Composer: Farshid Samandari

Shadow Catch
act iv

Daphne Marlatt

Farshid Samandari

Instrumental music. WAKI is at his spot,
looking around him.

Waiting song.

WAKI

This park I thought would shelter me
from shame and rage –
my dad's violence dogs me here,
it shadows me where
other shadows surround me.

JI

Other shadows surround me.

WAKI

Strangers full of their stories
recount their losses,
prompt me to engage with them.
I see them shadowed too
by shame, guilt, and blame. Is there
nowhere free from this?

Entrance music. SHITE appears as a battered
drunk, holding a bottle. As he sings his way
down the path approaching WAKI, he waves the
bottle at him.

SHITE

Ha, there is always
nowhere to run to if
you're a nobody
so why not settle for a swallow
from a nobody's
bottle and forget no one
will tell no one here
who you are.

Spoken dialogue.

WAKI

Another one! Well, mister, if you've got a story you'd better
spill it now. The night's almost over.

SHITE

Nobody has no story left. They're all leftovers anyway. But
they invent one when I'm on the beat. What's yours?

WAKI

I don't have a story I want to tell.

SHITE

Go on, kid, you're full of yourself. You think you're somebody,
don't you?

WAKI

No, I don't. Since I've ended up here, I'm just a pair of ears.

SHITE

Ah, plainclothes are you? A spotter? A narc? Who're you working for?

WAKI

I don't know anybody, I'm new in town.

SHITE

You young guys, all you wannabe somebodies, you think you're so smart. But you're nobody in an instant. (*pointing his bottle at WAKI*) One little bang and you're nothin', ya hear? I know who you are, you're one of them agitators, you're a commie.

WAKI

You sound as crazy as my dad. I don't know what you're talking about.

SHITE

Asshole! I was Detective Sergeant, knew all the bookies and bootleggers in town, I know what's what.

> *Memory song.* **SHITE** *begins to transform into a threatening young policeman as the story of the Battle of Ballantyne Pier unfolds.*

SHITE

Eager I was,
an East End kid wanting out.
Chief Foster's training
brought me up, a mounted cop
sittin' young and proud
atop my horse
with the force at Ballantyne.

JI

Foster warned you rabble,
you no-good strikers with your
ex-servicemen
sympathizers, tin-canners all.

SHITE

We held the tracks, we
beat you back from the dock.

JI

Despite your rain of rocks
with tear-gas fire, we beat you back
up narrow alleys,
batons a-whack, up front steps
of houses and shops,

SHITE

We cracked your heads you dirty
commie radicals.

Spoken dialogue.

WAKI

(*placating*) Okay, okay. So you're a cop, or you were. When was that?

SHITE

(*with less bravado*) Depression time. That was tough, kid, tough. Agitators, unrest, riots, snake parades. Hobo jungles you wouldn't want to step in. War cleared them out. Post war, this town was swinging again, if you know what I mean.

WAKI

I don't know what you mean.

SHITE

(*bragging again*) Bottle hawkers, under-the-table clubs, secret numbers games. East End crawling with bookies, bootleggers, hooker hotels. Ripe for the picking. Foster was gone, it was Mulligan now, and we were up for it, the pickings I mean.

Continued memory song, mimed with bravado.

SHITE

Smart new house in Kerrisdale
fur coat for the wife
cabinets full of the best
liquor money would,
and secrecy could,
buy.
Status I had, head of the
gambling unit, five

men working under me.
I was somebody
to reckon with. I was
Somebody, kid.

WAKI

So what happened?

SHITE stops and turns on WAKI.

SHITE

Framed. Liars framed me,
envious scum,
those bastards hankering for
what I had, they forced me out –
Young scum like you!

*SHITE begins to advance on WAKI with
bottle raised.*

WAKI

Hey! Chill out! I had
nothing to do with what
happened to you.

SHITE

You lousy commie,
swearing up and down you don't
know nothin' when I know
you're in deep, you're in shit, boy
right up to your lying eyes.

*SHITE punches the air between them, then
turns on imaginary opponents.*

WAKI

(*falling back*) My "lying eyes"?
That's what he'd say, the very
words he'd yell before
he'd beat me with his fuckin' belt.
Now I see who you are ...

> *WAKI steps forward as if to confront SHITE.
> But SHITE is shadowboxing by himself.*

JI

"You no-good asshole!"
Father flashes before him
in violent fury,
the beating, raging
accusations from
a twisted mind, furious
blows the boy has tried
to leave behind.

WAKI

This shadow catches me up,

JI

Catches me out, my
shadow attached to me.

SHITE

(*turning on WAKI*) You lousy nobody!

SHITE and JI

I'll beat you back all the way
across the tracks
I'll beat you back...

> *SHITE makes a sudden threatening leap
> towards WAKI, who stops him with his hand
> up, a hand of concentrated energy.*

WAKI

Hey! Do you see where you are?
Right back where you started from,
this old East End park you thought
you'd left behind.

> *SHITE steps back from WAKI, his anger
> collapsing into defeat.*

WAKI

Your shadow haunts you as mine
haunts me in this place,
this night so full of loss.

JI

Yet, and yet –

WAKI

I hear your story, old man.
I hear you in reverse
inside my ears that have been beaten,
on my shoulders, in my hands...

SHITE

You mean...?

WAKI

Your story tells me who I am.

SHITE

A nobody's son.

WAKI

A nobody's son...

SHITE

We're all nobodies here
trying to be Somebody.
In the end we'll disappear –
just so you know, kid.

JI

Yet, and yet...

SHITE

> I thought I could be
> Somebody. Right there was where
> I struck out.

> > *SHITE shrinks back into a derelict, shakes*
> > *his head, embarrassed at his own words, then*
> > *shuffles off to the JI bench.*

JI

> He caught himself outside
> his story he was deep inside.

WAKI

> Caught myself outside
> my own inside so fraught I
> wanted out. His story
> shows me there is nowhere
> else to be,

JI

> *inside that outside*
> *outside that in*

> all our lives so transient
> with darkness in them,
> dark that must be met.

WAKI

> Catch that shadow,
> caught it in passing!

*JI rises and moves downstage to join WAKI as
JI members chant, each one in turn:*

JI

K'emk'emeláẏ
Paueru Groundo
Oppenheimer
Powell Street Grounds

JI

all together
the nameless rhythm ground

WAKI

all interleafed

JI

all together
those long gone and here

WAKI

all interleafing here

These last two lines are sung together.

THE END

Kevin Kiho Sohn as the Waki in *Shadow Catch* at the Old Auditorium, UBC, March 12, 2022.

Photo by Sarah Race.

Katie Fraser as the Spirit of the Maple Trees in *Shadow Catch* at the Old Auditorium, UBC, March 13, 2022.

Photo by Sarah Race.

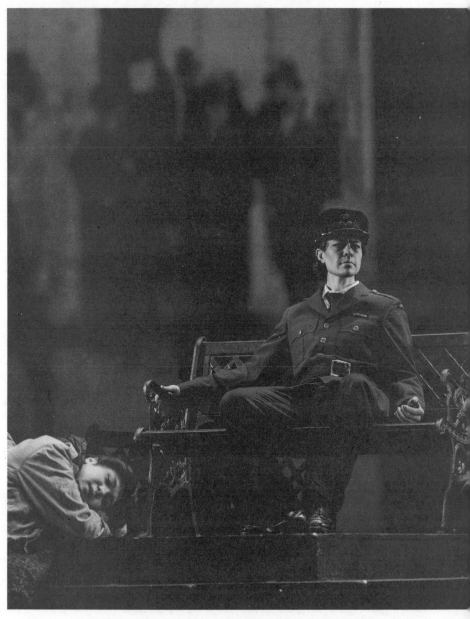

Matthew McLellan as the Spirit of the Police Officer in *Shadow Catch* at the Old Auditorium, UBC, March 12, 2022.

Photo by Sarah Race.

Rachel Buttress as the Spirit of the Brothel Madam in *Shadow Catch* at the Old Auditorium, UBC, March 12, 2022.

Photo by Sarah Race.

Luka Kawabata as the Spirit of the Asahi Baseball Player in *Shadow Catch* at the Old Auditorium, UBC, March 12, 2022.

Photo by Sarah Race.

Historical Background

Melanie Adams as the Spirit of the Maple Trees in *Shadow Catch* at the Firehall Theatre, December 2011.

Photo by Timothy Matheson.

Act 1

Bigleaf Maples

Long before the area of Vancouver where *Shadow Catch* is set was known as the Downtown Eastside, it was a gathering and harvesting place for the xʷməθkʷəy̓əm (Musqueam), S̱ḵwx̱wú7mesh (Squamish), səl̓ilwətaʔɫ (Tsleil-Waututh), and Stó:lō Peoples. S̱ḵwx̱wú7mesh people know it as K̓emk̓emeláy̓ – "the place of many maple trees" – because of the bigleaf maple trees that flourished there, as in what's now known as Oppenheimer Park.

The preferred habitat of the barred owl, bigleaf maples provide food and habitat for a host of creatures, functioning as a community hub or gathering space for humans and non-humans alike. They produce winged seeds which squirrels, grosbeaks, and other animals eat; their large leaves provide a shady canopy for many creatures and food for deer, elk, beavers, and others; and, of course, they are a source of wood. Bigleaf maples were among the trees logged and processed at mills established up and down the coast after the arrival of European settlers – mills such as Hasting Mill, where Indigenous workers were employed alongside Japanese, Chinese, Yugoslav, Scandinavian, and African ones. As a result of overharvesting, there are now reportedly only two remaining bigleaf maples in K̓emk̓emeláy̓, a devastating loss for the whole interconnected community they once supported.

Photographer unknown, *Invincible Asahis, taken at Powell Street Grounds,* 1926, Nikkei National Museum, 2010.17.1.55

Photographer unknown, *The Last Asahis,* 1941, Nikkei National Museum, 2010.26.19

Act 2

The Asahi Baseball Team

by Jason Beck, curator at the BC Sports Hall of Fame

If not for the extraordinary passion of a few former players, spectators, and their families, the memory of the Vancouver Asahi baseball team – one of Vancouver's most prominent athletic clubs in the interwar period – very likely would have been lost forever. Only recently has the impact of this club on the Japanese community and the larger sporting community in BC been truly appreciated.

The Asahi (meaning "morning sun") ball club was formed in 1914 under the leadership of a Powell Street dry cleaner named Harry Miyasaki, who wanted a team that could defeat the hard-hitting Anglo Canadian ball clubs and win the Terminal League championship.

In 1926, Miyasaki got his wish as the Asahi won the Terminal League playoffs and were voted most popular team in the city. The accolades continued in ensuing years, with Terminal League championships in 1930 and 1933, a run of Pacific Northwest championships from 1937 to 1941, and a triple-championship season in 1938: Burrard, Commercial, and Pacific Northwest. The club developed a farm system with as many as four teams to identify young talent that might someday play for the senior team – many young boys' dream in Vancouver's Little Tokyo community.

The Asahi developed their own unique style of play that endeared them to most spectators, including many Anglo Canadians. The players tended to be smaller and less powerful hitters than those on Anglo ball teams, so the Asahi relied on speed, defence, and smarts – "brain ball," they called it. One of the trademarks of the Asahi became their success using the squeeze play to get men on base and move them to the "next station" on the base paths, one bunt at a time. In 1927, the Asahi won a game 3–1 without technically collecting a single hit – bunts, steals, and opposition errors were all the Asahi required to win on that amazing afternoon.

In 1941, the Asahi ball club disbanded, never to be reformed. The Canadian reaction to the bombing of Pearl Harbor led to the forced relocation of all Japanese Canadians into various internment camps in the interior of the province, with most of their property and possessions confiscated forever.

The team was irrevocably lost, but the Asahi remained a beacon of hope in an incredibly dark and trying time. The former players, despite being scattered among the many camps, formed teams with whatever players were available. Teams from different camps began playing one another informally, leading to the formation of the Slocan Valley championship. The game became a morale booster for an uprooted people unfairly confined by the harsh policies of a paranoid government. Where Asahi baseball had previously given Japanese Canadians a sense of pride, the team now grew to near-mythic proportions within the Japanese Canadian community, as the on-field deeds of great players such as Kaz Suga and Kaye Kaminishi were recounted and debated. In 1945, the disbandment of the internment camps forced many former Asahi players to scatter across the country.

In June 2003, the Vancouver Asahi baseball team was finally accorded proper recognition for its contribution to Canadian baseball by induction into the Canadian Baseball Hall of Fame. A longstanding oversight was thus corrected and has only been more firmly righted with the team's induction into the BC Sports Hall of Fame in 2005.

The proud name that had instilled such spirit and hope into its people – Asahi – will not be forgotten.

Act 3

Vancouver's Former Red-Light District

by Lani Russwurm

The first known brothel in the Vancouver Downtown Eastside was Birdie Stewart's house on Water Street near Abbott Street, which opened in 1873. In the 1880s, Chinese Canadian residents established their own settlement on the north shore of False Creek, then on the margins of Vancouver. For the anglophiles steering Vancouver's development, the sex trade also belonged on the margins, so Dupont Street, Chinatown's main drag, doubled as a red-light district. Vancouver grew rapidly after incorporation in 1886, and by the turn of the twentieth century, Chinatown was closer to the city centre than to the outskirts. In 1902 Vancouver also had a new, moral-reform-minded mayor, Thomas Neelands, who set out to "clean up" his "vice-ridden" city.

When the crackdown on Dupont Street brothels began in 1906, the red-light district shifted to two small lanes off Dupont: Canton Alley and Shanghai Alley. The 1906 campaign to clear bawdy houses from Dupont Street and Shanghai and Canton Alleys failed, and the city's madams were allowed to set up shop on a half-block stretch of Harris Street (now East Georgia Street) between Westminster Avenue (now Main Street) and False Creek. To avoid embarrassing the more "respectable" Harris Street residents to the east, it was renamed Shore Street in 1908. Finally, in 1913, construction of

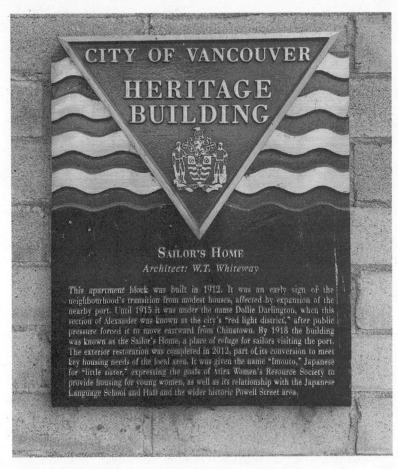

CITY OF VANCOUVER

HERITAGE BUILDING

SAILOR'S HOME
Architect: W.T. Whiteway

This apartment block was built in 1912. It was an early sign of the neighbourhood's transition from modest houses, affected by expansion of the nearby port. Until 1915 it was under the name Dollie Darlington, when this section of Alexander was known as the city's "red light district," after public pressure forced it to move eastward from Chinatown. By 1918 the building was known as the Sailor's Home, a place of refuge for sailors visiting the port. The exterior restoration was completed in 2012, part of its conversion to meet key housing needs of the local area. It was given the name "Imouto," Japanese for "little sister," expressing the goals of Atira Women's Resource Society to provide housing for young women, as well as its relationship with the Japanese Language School and Hall and the wider historic Powell Street area.

Karis Shearer, *Sailor's Home, Alexander St.*, 2022

the first Georgia Viaduct obliterated Shore Street. The red-light district had already begun the move to Alexander Street, in what was then part of Japantown, the previous year. Several of the purpose-built brothels can still be seen on Alexander Street, though now they serve as affordable, supportive housing for some of the most marginalized Vancouverites. The buildings constructed as brothels were essentially rooming houses, but fancier. Instead of a store or bar on the ground floor, they had a bar and lounge, and often a piano player to entertain guests. The only known photo of Shore Street shows that the buildings there were a step up from the rickety wooden structures on Dupont. The ones on Alexander Street were even gaudier, reflecting the prosperity of the madams.

Soon after the red-light district relocated to Alexander Street, moral reformers campaigned to shut it down. By the time war broke out in 1914, the city had declared that the red-light district was closed. Since then, the debate over how to handle the urban sex trade has continued unresolved, but there have been no other red-light districts sanctioned by the City of Vancouver.

Adapted from Lani Russwurm, "A History of Sex Work in Early Vancouver," forbiddenvancouver.ca/blog/history-prostitution-vancouver/.

J.S. Matthews, *Police Dispersing a Crowd during the Powell Street Riot*, City of Vancouver Archives, CVA 371-1127

Act 4

Class War: The Battle of Ballantyne Pier

by Michael Barnholden

On June 18, 1935, one thousand striking, locked-out longshoremen and their supporters began marching towards the Heatley Avenue entrance to Ballantyne Pier, where they were met by several hundred armed policemen. When the strikers, in order to prevent scabs from doing their jobs, approached the police lines, Vancouver Police Chief Constable Colonel W.W. Foster ordered them to disperse. When the workers tried to break through police lines, tear gas was deployed in Vancouver for the first but certainly not last time. Specially trained police officers, wearing gas masks, turned the workers back, and the Mounted Squad charged and beat the unarmed men with billy clubs. The workers fought back with stones and bricks and whatever else they could find.

Immediately dubbed "The Battle of Ballantyne Pier" by the local newspapers, it is hard to avoid the military implications of this episode in the class wars of Depression-era Vancouver. The workers marched led by disabled veteran and waterfront worker Mickey O'Rourke, recipient of the Victoria Cross, wearing his medals and carrying a Union Jack. Chief Constable Foster had been recently hired to "modernize the VPD," which to him meant militarization: more martial uniforms and the use of chemical warfare and machine guns in preparation for what Mayor Gerald

McGeer was predicting – a Bolshevik revolution, led by members of the Worker's Unity League, a Communist Party of Canada front, who were well represented on the battle line.

Not represented on the battle line, at least not in person, were the members of the Citizen's League, who paid for the training and equipment of 160 "Specials." The Citizens League was a front organization for the Shipping Federation. As the managing director of the timber-exporting company Evans, Coleman and Evans, Colonel Foster had been asked to head the Shipping Federation's Protection Committee during the 1923 longshoremen's strike. That strike was broken and the union was replaced by a new company union, the Vancouver and District Waterfront Workers' Association. By 1935 this union's leadership had become radicalized and were at the forefront in the proposed general strike; they saw the confrontation at Ballantyne Pier as part of their attempt to bargain for better wages, safer working conditions, and a call-out system that would respect seniority rather than employer favouritism.

Acknowledgments

Heartfelt gratitude to my editor Catriona Strang, who helped enormously to find historical photographs and gather historical background for Oppenheimer Park, as well as pages from each of the composer's scores for this book.

Also my gratitude, as always, to Les Smith for his inspired book design and his patience.

Thanks again to Ellie Nichol for permission to quote the lines "inside that outside / outside that in" from bpNichol's "for steve" in his collection *Zygal: A Book of Mysteries and Translations* (Coach House Press, 1985).

Continuing gratitude to Colleen Lanki for her Noh Arts organizing, her direction, and her dance and Noh performances that have brought the classical traditions of Japanese Noh and Kabuki theatre to life in Vancouver. My gratitude also to composers Benton Roark, Dorothy Chang, Jennifer Butler, and Farshid Samandari, whose musical skills combined with their innovative spirit created such a moving score for *Shadow Catch*.

My thanks to Firehall Theatre's Donna Spencer for welcoming the first production of *Shadow Catch* there in 2011. And continuing thanks to Nancy Hermiston for organizing and directing UBC Opera's remarkable production in 2022.

As always, longstanding gratitude to Tokyo-based Richard Emmert of Theatre Nohgaku, gifted Noh musician, performer, and organizer in the West of further Noh knowledge and innovation.

Further thanks to Susan Knutson for her continuing interest in and insightful critical article about *Shadow Catch* in *Modern Drama* 62, no. 2 (2019): 149–170.

This libretto would not have been written without the continual love, patience, and understanding of Bridget MacKenzie.

Shadow Catch librettist and composers on the set of the 2011 Firehall Theatre production.

Standing, left to right: Daphne Marlatt, Dorothy Chang

Seated, left to right: Jennifer Butler, Benton Roark, Farshid Samandari

Photo by Timothy Matheson.

Born in Australia, Vancouver poet **DAPHNE MARLATT** immigrated to Canada from Penang, Malaysia, as a child in 1951. She is a critically acclaimed poet and novelist whose cross-genre work has been translated into French and Dutch. The bicultural production of her Canadian Noh play, *The Gull*, received the 2008 international Uchimura Naoya Prize. Her long poem in prose fragments, *The Given*, won the 2009 Dorothy Livesay Award. In 2005 she was appointed to the Order of Canada and in 2012 received the George Woodcock Lifetime Achievement Award. Her recent poetry titles include *Liquidities: Vancouver Poems Then and Now* (2013), *Rivering: The Poetry of Daphne Marlatt*, edited by Susan Knutson (2014), *Reading Sveva* (2016), *Intertidal: Collected Earlier Poems, 1968–2008*, edited by Susan Holbrook (2017), and *Then Now* (2021).